# *Words to Live By; Lessons Learned*

## *Carolyn M. Ellison*

# Words to Live By; Lessons Learned

ISBN-13: 978-0615619446

Scripture references are from the King James Version.

**Printed in the United States of America**

**Published by**

**Testimony of Life Publications**

## *Dedication*

This book is dedicated to my Heavenly Father, my Lord and Savior Jesus Christ. It's my life mission to spread *His w*ord.

My family, my children, my grandchildren.

My prayer partners at Palmetto Health, Ruth, Mary, Demetria, Rose, Hope, Shannon and Jessie Yarborough,

My many editors, Mrs. Marvina Green, Cheryl Apodaca, Jerlean Noble, the President of Columbia Writer Alliance and my cousin Monica Jenkins. Stephanie Suell and a Big thanks to Mr. Kyle Sutton, for encouraging me to start my publishing Company (Testimony for Life).

## *Foreword*

"If it was not for Carolyn Ellison and her constant teachings and references to the Bible in real life time, I would not know where to turn. We met as co-workers at Palmetto Health and are prayer partners for morning review of the troubles that are faced by us, family, our co-workers and friends that have a struggle with life and the guidelines to follow in life. If you follow the guidelines of this book and make a Jump (Jesus understands my troubles) and a leap of faith, it is surely going to lead you in the right direction."

*~Ruth Melissa Cornell~*

# Preface

The moment you are pushed out of your mother's womb, life begins. After a long and tiring process, you made it! Welcome to the world! You can now breathe on your own.

Welcome to earth! A home once called paradise until the fall of man (Adam). Adam and Eve lived in perfect harmony with God in the Garden of Eden. Imagine a perfect place with no dying, hatred, sickness or disease. A place where only God's love reigns.

In the garden, along with Adam and Eve, lived the evil serpent. The serpent only had one thing on his mind...revenge for God tossing him out of heaven. Like Adam, the devil had a free will to think and his thinking was evil.

Adam and Eve did not use the mind which God gave them! This is why the devil was able to deceive them into committing the most deadliest sin. God prohibited them from eating off the tree of Knowledge of Good and Evil, yet they disobeyed God's warning.. They had several options to choose from and they chose the wrong one.

Due to the fact Adam and Eve did not think before they reacted, both of their eyes were opened to sin. They knew they were naked and they hid from God. Adam didn't listen to God's warning about eating from the tree of good and evil. He was hardheaded and didn't listen to the voice of love. He let the devil trick his mind, and reacted of his own free will. Adam passed his sin down to all of mankind. From Adam's disobedience, we all wear the scars of sin. Adam's sin separated us from God.

### *Genesis 3*

God created this place we call home for mankind to live happily. However, because of sin, we live in a world that is full of corruption, hatred and bigotry. A world where we constantly ask "Where is the love?" God is love! He is the creator of heaven and earth. The one who sent his only son into the world to redeem mankind from their sin. Freely giving them the choice to be free from their sins, and to live according to God's word, which is the righteous way. Where has the love gone? **John 3:16**

*How do we get back to the plans God has for man?*

*It all starts in the mind. How we think will bring meaning to life...***Romans 12:2**

From the moment you enter this world your life starts.

When Jesus walked this earth as a man, he was a student. His earthly parents, Mary and Joseph were God fearing. They taught their son the ways of the Lord. Joseph taught his son, Jesus, how to be a carpenter.

As a boy, Jesus had a hunger and thirst to be about God's business. He would sit in the temple and listen to the teachers. Jesus grew and became strong. He was filled with wisdom and the grace of God was upon Him.

**Luke 2:40-51**

When it was promotion time for Jesus, a voice spoke down from heaven saying, "This is my Son, whom I love; with him I am well pleased." **Matthew 3:17**

It is important that a child learns from home first. What that child learns will carry with them throughout their life. The life lessons they learn will help them live either prosperous or defeated lives. If we raise children up in the way God said we should, they may stray from the word; however, they will come back. When God's word is in their heart, it's hard to forget. God won't let you forget when the word is rooted within. Use what you know, to do right. The choice is yours. **Proverbs 22**

Life is a journey and yes, life is hard. The hardest thing about this journey is walking without God.

Oh! If I could turn back the hands of time to all of my bad decisions, I would have thought things through before I reacted. I would not have just reacted first! How many times have those words came out of your mouth? We cannot dwell on the past. If we do, we will never embrace the future.

The purpose of life's lessons are to teach not repeat. If mankind benefits from your lessons, that will prevent them from following in your shoes. Thank God for the lessons you've learned.

Before Abraham would become the father of many nations, God had to change Abraham's way of thinking. He could not be a father that taught his children to worship idols and to tell lies. Abraham had to learn to do things God's way and to live by God's plan. The nations depended on his teachings. **Genesis 17:5**

To see change, be the change you want to see. Change is a daily process. God is not going to force you to change, your heart has to be willing to change. You have to stop doing the things that caused you to think and act in ungodly ways. You have to view people, places, and things from God's standpoint. Change does not happen overnight. You did not become who you are overnight, and it's going take more time for God to change you. God created the earth in six days, not one.

When God is ready to use us for His glory, *He* will take us through an inspection before *He* places our life on display. People will be watching to see if what you say and how you live corresponds with the word of God. God used Abraham's life to change nations. God can do the same for you, if you let *Him* be your teacher.

# Table of Contents

## *The Bible*

Life is a journey
It requires direction
If you don't know where you came from
How do you know where you are going?
The
**B**asic
**I**nstruction 4
**B**asic
**L**ife
**E**vents
Use the *Light* to guide you where you need to go.


*2 Timothy 3:16-17*
*Matthew 7:2*

# *He Gave Me A Way Out*

A voice cries within
How do I get out?
No one I can talk to,
Who would understand my pain?
My diagnosis
Misunderstood
You touched my mouth,
Now I can speak
Pen in my hand
Dips of ink
Our faces meet
Let's talk.

***Jeremiah 1:9***

# Obedience Is Better Than Sacrifice

I heard the word
I applied the word
I am blessed by the word
For being obedient to the word
I now spread the word.

*James 1:23*
*1 Samuel 15:22*

# Commitment/Relationship

When Jesus comes into your heart; you and *He* became bone of bone and flesh of flesh. You and God become one. You make a sacred **vow**: to **love, honor** and **obey His words**. God promises that *He* will never leave or forsake you; even death won't separate you from the Lord. To be absent from the body is to be present with the Lord.

The **vows** you and your husband made to each other are the same vows you made to God. You made a **commitment** to **love,** trust, through sickness, hardship and death.

Marriage is not **easy**. It does require **work**, from both the bride and the groom. Don't let life's problems end your marriage with God. You are not alone. If God be for you, no man can be against you. When the going gets tough, you get tougher. Remember the **vow** you made. You will never see what the end will bring, if you give up.

# *The Commitment*

It's a beautiful summer Saturday afternoon.

The sun is bright, the sky is blue.

What a day to get married!

At the altar,

wearing a smile that warms the room,

the groom awaits his bride.

Music softly plays

She slowly enters the room.

Walking down the aisle with Dad

She sees family and friends,

who come to witness this blessed union.

She thinks,

"Once I say I do"

Its official

I choose to take this man to be my rib

Committed to spend the rest of my life

I am no longer my own.

He and I will become one.

The walk stops

She approaches her soon to be husband.

The father lets go of his daughter.

Bride and groom turn to face the preacher

# The Commitment(Continued)

Happiness and joy on their faces

"Will you take this woman to be your wife?"

"Yes"

"Will you take this man to be your husband?"

"Yes".

"I now pronounce you man and wife."

The commitment is sealed with a kiss.

***Ephesians 5:22-33***

# *Invitation Only*

God is knocking at your heart,
He only comes in through your invite
God doesn't take
He freely gives
A time will come when the knocking will stop
Seek the Lord
While He is still near.

**Revelation 3:20**
**John 10:10**
**Isaiah 55:6**

# *What You Are Going Though*
# *Only God Can Save You*

Before you came into my life,
I did not want to live,
My life was dark and empty
I was hopeless.
Trying to care for two babies
I was in need of help.
My soul was drowning in my tears
How can I escape so much pain?
No one to reach out to
Who would understand what I was going through?
How could they?
When I did not understand myself?
My pain deeply rooted
How do I get to this place you call peace?
You promised
You found me
You heard my cry.
You heard my prayer.
You felt my pain
You came to my rescue.

*Exodus 2:23*

# The Gift of Life You Gave To Me

That day I gave my life to you
I didn't know what to expect
Life for me was not easy
I was tired of doing things my way.
So I tried your way
So glad I did
You gave me a brand new start
All my sin was washed away
Tossed in the sea of no return
You gave me the gift of life.
No greater love.

*2 Corinthians 5:17*
*Psalm 103:12*
*Romans 5:8*

# *Faith*

We must believe there is a God to have **faith**. **Faith** is not what we see; **Faith** is what we believe. **Without faith** it is impossible to please God. How do we get **Faith**? **Faith** comes by **hearing** and **hearing** comes from the **word of God**.

The mind is the battlefield for the devil to attack our thoughts. If we don't have the fuel to fight him back, the enemy will chew us up and spit us out. To survive the devil's attacks, we need to be in the overflow of God's words. When we are equipped with what we need, no **weapon** formed against us, made by man, can hurt or stop what God has for us. Stand in faith.

*We may not see our vision in the natural, but we can say with* ***confidence****, "I have what I trust God to bring to my life."*

A woman goes to the doctor because she believes she is pregnant. He confirms what she already knew. She cannot wait to get an ultrasound to see her baby. When she goes in for the ultrasound, she gets a glance of her baby for the first time. This tiny **seed** God has planted inside her womb is the **reality** of her vision. Nine months later she is holding her baby. If God gives you a vision, trust and believe it shall come to path.

**Faith** says, "You can have all the success you want; if you only put your trust in God." There is no limit to what God can do. What He has done for others, *He* can do the same for you. How do you think President Obama became the first black president of the United States? He trusted God; kept **faith** in God; and his **faith** said, "Yes I can."

You will never see your dream, goals, or anything, come to **reality,** if you don't put your faith in God and believe. **He can do all things.** Stand still and watch the Lord bring your vision to life.

*Hebrews 11:1-3*
*Romans 10:17*
*Hebrews 11:6*

# Don't Believe What You See, Believe What It Is Going Be

It is cold
Dark
I feel all alone
Where are you?
My human eyes are getting the victory
I am scared
I don't know the outcome
I know it's only a test
I put my faith in you
You promise that I will survive
If I put my trust in you
Help me to walk by faith
Not by sight.

*James 2:17*
*2 Corinthians 5:7*

# "If God Said It"
## That's Enough For Me

How do you believe?
When He says, "Trust me"
Your life is in disarray,
How do you believe?
When He says, "I will never leave you"
Loved ones have forsaken you,
How do you believe?
When He says, "I will supply all your needs"
You struggle to pay your bills,
How do you believe?
When He says, "By my stripes you are healed"
You have a blood clot in your lung,
How do you believe the unseen?
That says,
"Walk by faith not by sight"?
If God said it
That settles it!

*Numbers 23:19*

# *See-Saw Faith*

Through much opposition
I perceived, and yes, I believed I would fail.
The tests He allowed me to go through
Divorce, depression, and rejection
Although, I couldn't see God,
I knew He was there.
Everlasting peace He gives
Through it all
He is my shield.

**Psalm 18:2**

# *Walk By Faith*
# *Not By Fear*

I have to admit,
Trusting you wasn't easy.
Fear had me paralyzed
From the bondage that held me captive.
After many test and trials,
I came to the decision, it was either do or die!
I shall live and not die.
You delivered me from the hand of my enemy.
You have proven your love to me.

.

**Psalm 118:17**

# *I Know What He Said*

When thoughts
Try to consume my mind,
I'm reminded of Your Word.
I walk by faith
Not by sight.
I refuse to give in
I know the promise
Plans to prosper and not harm me.
You said, if I keep the faith,
fight a good fight.
I have a prize that awaits me.
You told me
If I don't give in and never doubt
You will bless me.


***2 Corinthians 10:5***

# *You Can't Take Away My Faith*

All I have is my faith.
You tried to take my mind;
God wouldn't let it be.
Test and trials come to make me strong.
My faith is the reason I still hold on.
You can take everything from me.
You cannot take away my faith
Through my storms, my faith increased;
Through my trials, I learned how to wait on God.

*James 1:12*
*James1-8*

# *He Is Afraid Of You*

The devil is scared too.

He knows his kingdom is about to succumb.

Why do you think he fights you so hard?

You are a thorn in his flesh;

He knows his outcome.

If you ever get the vision, of what God has ordained for your life,

You will not work for the devil.

He will be working for you.

The devil is no threat

He is a foot stool, to your destiny.

*Revelation 20:10*
*Matthew 22:44*

# My Gifts Will Make Room for Me

Everything good and perfect comes from above.
I have been given power to possess what's on the inside.
All these gifts birthed in me;
Only I can bring them to life.
Abundance of Love
Innocence
Testimony for Life
Many other Gifts not revealed yet.
They are the evidence I don't see
God's hope lives inside me.


*James 1:17*
*Proverbs 18:16*

# *It's Time to Step Out of the Boat*

It's time for me to step out and fulfill my destiny.
God's given me visions only I can achieve
By taking a leap of faith.
God has equipped me to make a difference.
The devil is on my track
With all his lies
I refuse to believe.
No longer will I run and hide.
I will use the gifts inside
To tell the world
How great is our God.

*Matthew 14:22-33*
*2 Timothy 3:17*
*Psalm 40:10*

## *Change: Let God Transform Your Mind*

The minute you become a born again Christian, I believe your process starts. You have given God permission to **renew your mind**. **Change** doesn't happen overnight. You did not become who you are overnight, and it's not going take overnight for God to **change** you. God created the earth in **six days**.

Being a born again Christian doesn't make you perfect. Our mind must be **conformed** from our old way of thinking and let God **transform** us to think His way. You have to stop doing things that caused you to think and act in ungodly ways. People, places, and things ... you have to view them from **God's standpoint**.

**Change** is a daily process. As long as God's blood runs in the body, and His air breathes through your lungs, you can change. You say, "I have faith." Faith is not enough. You and God have to work together. God is not going to force you to change; your **heart** has to be **willing**. You have to **activate** your faith; you must have a lifestyle **change**. It's time God cleaned your closet.

*Romans 12:1-2*

# *You Be the Change*

I asked God to change my family.

He said, "No I am changing you.

You heard my voice, and you answered me.

I transform the mind that will make your life brand new.

When I change you,

People have to adapt to the change I made in you.

No longer carnal minded

My spirit lives in you."

***Romans 8:9***
***Matthew 5:14-16***

# *Your Change Is Your Change*

Don't expect people to change when you change
Don't expect people to believe your change,
You didn't become who you are overnight
It is not going take God overnight to change you
God created the earth in six days
It is a process
Your walk is your walk
When others decide to walk with God that will be there walk
Before your change, the **old** person they knew
Allow People time, to get to know the **new** you.

*John 6:44*
*2 Corinthians 5:17*

# *You Don't Have The Right To Throw Stones*

Nobody's perfect
We are all sinners saved by grace
Not by any work we do
You don't have the right to throw stones
Before God saved you
You were a sinner who was saved by grace.

*Ephesians 2:8*
*John 8:7*
*Romans 3:23*

# God Lives On The Inside

When God renews your mind; He has to dissect you from **within**. To make sure you line up with **His word**. God is the head and we are the many parts to His body; we should all be in **unity** as we follow Christ. God will take us through an **inspection** before He places us on **display**. Before the twelve disciples were released to evangelize, they went through extensive training with Jesus. They **learned** how to act, talk and walk like Jesus.

People will be watching you, to see if your **mouth** and **life** line up with the **word of God**. There should be no confusion as to who is leading you. If there is something inside of you not producing the image of Christ, He has to go **inside** and get rid of the waste that is causing you to produce **bad fruit**; so He can produce **good fruit**. People will know the God in you by the **good fruit** you **produce.** Everything has to work in **unity** so many can see the **good change** God has done in your life so; you can serve as a **witness** for Christ.

*Romans 8:28*
*Matthew 12:33*
*Matthew 5:16*

# When God Goes Inside,
## He Looks for Himself

**Respiratory-** it is God's air we breathe,
He breathes life into us.
We should treat every breath
As if it is our last breath.  ***Genesis 2:7***

**Heart-** God has to check your heart to see if your love is genuine
for Him and your neighbor.  ***Luke 10:27***

**Brain-** God checks our brain
To see if we have a mind like Christ.  ***2 Corinthians 5:17***

**Nervous system-** God has to make sure we
send out the right message
when we are witnessing for Him.  ***Mark 16:15***

**Eyes-** God has to check our eyes
To see if the light leads you.  ***John 8:12; Matthew 6:22***

**Digestive system-** God has to prune out bad fruit; to produce good
fruit.
(Jealousy, gossip, anger).

***John 15:1-17***
***Galatians 5:22-23***

# Seasons –
# Life Changes

There will be **seasons** in your life that require God to take you through some uncomfortable things. During these times you might want to give up. You might say if being saved is all this; being broke, sick and lonely, God can have this saved life. When I lived in sin, life was hard, but the taste of sin I enjoyed. When a bill was due, one call and it was paid. At what price?

With the devil, there is always a price to pay behind his so-called blessing. You have to take a lot to get his blessing. Many times you might get called a name that is not godly, or you might get physically abused. With him nothing comes free.

How many **times** has God kept you from death? How many **times** has God kept you in whatever **season** you were in?

You can be so close to your **season change**; your **breakthrough**, that once you look back, you will be stuck in unbelief. If you give up, what do you have to go back to? With God no matter what **season** you're in, you are coming out. That's a promise you can bank on. You have to know what seasons you're in so God can do in you and through you, to bring other **seasons** that He wants to bless you in. When you know what **season** you are in, it helps you embrace the **change**...

*Ecclesiastes 3:8*

# *God's Word Never Changes*

Winter, Spring, Summer and fall,
God made all.
April Shower,
May Flower,
Spring is here.
Get ready for the sweet taste of summer;
No more school.
Welcome
Hundred degree weather
Those hot summer days have all faded away.
Now is the time to put all these summer clothes away,
Bring out clothes that will be warm to the chill.
Fall is the time when we know the fair is near.
A time we look forward to the cotton candy,
Candy apples… Oh what a treat.
When the fair has come and gone,
The leaves turn brown and gold.
When the air has turned windy and cold,
We know Thanksgiving is near.
A time family and friends come together,
A time we should give thanks every day,
Not just once a year.

# God's Word Never Changes(Continued)

Gathering around the table with turkey, dressing, and oh yes!
Grandma's homemade sweet potato pie!
As the air gets colder and colder
We know what comes next,
That great day we all expect, December 25th,
The day we celebrate the birth
Of our Lord and Savior, Jesus Christ.
Though seasons might come and go
There is one thing you can surely depend on.
The word of God will never Change
It will forever remain the same.

*Revelation 22:13*
*Hebrews 13:8*

# Deception-
## Don't Let Him Deceive You

Don't listen to his **lies**. It was the devil's lies that caused the world to be in sin. The devil comes to **steal, kill**, and **destroy**. He is a **liar**; He **cannot** tell the **truth**. He will use anybody or anything to **distract** you. He has no respect for you. What does he care about using your children, parents, and your finances against you? You have dumped him.

You are no longer with a **zero**. You are now with a hero. You left the zero relationship, and the feeling wasn't mutual. The devil wants you back. He needs your body to do his evil work and to make you feel worthless. He is a **coward**. That's why he needs you. Don't listen to the smooth talk. How much he loves you and misses you. When you resist him, he will leave you alone.

He will **tempt** you with **new schemes**. He doesn't have any **new tricks**. If you recognize his **scheme**, you will **beat** him at his own **game**.

He doesn't like your hero. Your hero makes you happy. He loves you unconditionally. You are not alone. Your hero will fight your battle. The **zero** doesn't have a **chance**.

*Ephesians 6:10-18*
*James 4:7*
*John 8:44*

# *Beware of the Lying Tongue*

Adam was God's child.
The apple of His father's eye.
God created a home,
The Garden of Eden,
For Adam and his wife, Eve.
They didn't have a care in the world;
As to what should I eat?
Or what should I wear?
As the cliché goes
Adam was born with a silver spoon in mouth.
Adam was given dominion over everything;
As long as He obeyed God's instruction
Not to eat from the Tree of good and evil.
Along with Adam and Eve,
There was the serpent,
Shrewder than any of the wild animals
He tricked Eve
With this question,
"Did God really say?
That you must not eat from the tree?
He doesn't want you to be like Him
Know Good and evil."
Being as deceptive as he was,
He convinced her to eat off the tree;
She gave Adam the apple, and he ate it too.
From that moment both eyes were open to sin.
The Sin of disobedience caused him to be put out of his home.
Adam's sin separates all people from God.   *Genesis 3*

# *Temporary Fix*

Don't stop the process
By depending on something that's man-made.
It only gives you a temporary stand still.
When the fix is over, the process still rolls on.
Allow God to take you through your process;
Allow opportunity for growth.
Something beautiful will happen,
Your life will change.

**Psalm 146:3**
**Psalm 4:5**

# *Choices-*
# *Make the Right Turn*

Life is a journey, and life is hard.  There are many **turns** that appear to be the **right road** to take.  When you go down these roads and you find the roads are not what you expect, there is no **peace** on the **wrong road**.  There are **two roads** that we will travel; the **right road** is narrow, and **few** will travel.  The **wrong road** is wide, **many** will travel.  Choose the **right road,** and you will live in **peace**.  Trust the Lord, let Him lead you to make the **right turn**.  **Jesus is the truth the way and the life. Jesus is the right turn.**

*Matthew 7:13*
*Proverbs 3:5-6*
*John 14:6*

# *The Choice Is Yours*

You choose your turn.
There is a right turn and a wrong turn,
It's up to you to decide the wrong turn leads to a path of destruction.
The right turn leads to eternal peace.
On your journey
Hard times make you strong.
It's what equips you to make the right turn.

*Proverbs 14:12*
*Proverbs 19:21*
*Proverbs 16:9*

# *Direction-*
# *Get Back On Track*

God has mapped out our life. It is up to you to stay on track. When we get off the **course** God has ordained for our lives, **stormy situations** happen. For God to get us **back on track** when these things happen, it's time for a **self-examination** check. We need to ask God what is it that you are not doing that causes your life to be on a spiral.

When a car needs an alignment the car speaks to you. It might not talk, but you know your car, you know how it's supposed to drive. That's the same way with God. **The Creator knows His creation.** Whatever God has to do to get your **attention**, He will allow it to get you back on track. He loves you. He doesn't want to see you **self destruct.**

*Jeremiah 29:11*
*Genesis 1:26*

# God Knew You
# Before You Were a Seed

God predestined your life;
He knew you
Before you were a seed.
"I know the plan
I have for you," says the Lord.
Plans to prosper you, and not harm you.
Plans for a good future.
Along the way, you got off course.
Now!  Bad things follow you.
Warning, warning!
God is speaking to you;
Check up time,
Your life is out of line...
You need to listen to God speak.

*Jeremiah 1:5*
*Psalm 139:16*

# Influence -
# Who Has Your Ear?

*Whoever has your ear that turns you away from God?* That's who you will serve; money, man, house and cars; *you have made your God.* How quickly we forget God when everything is going right in our lives.

When things go wrong in our lives, we're quick to call on God's name. God is not a yo-yo God. He is not an up and down God. God will get tired of your games and turn a deaf ear to your prayers until you choose what God you will serve. He is a jealous God.

*Proverbs 28:9*
*Matthew 6:24*
*Deuteronomy 4:24*

# Don't Forget the Hand
# That Brought You Out

Now that I helped you out
Everything's going alright.
This is how you repay me?
You give me your rear to kiss?
He did it to you,
I did it for you.
It was his lie that he told to get you in your stress.
Charming words that melt your heart
To get you do bad things.
He is the father of lies.
No truth in him.
It was I who hung on the cross.
It was my blood that saved you.
You forget me?
As quickly as I brought you out you'll enter back in.
Think twice by calling my name.
I may not be so swift to come to your rescue.
You may have to stay in the belly until you know better.
The next time you won't be so quick to forget my hand.

*Jeremiah 2*
*Deuteronomy 6:12*
*Isaiah 63:10*
*Jonah 2*

# Don't Take the Light Off of God

If God put you in a position
He is well able to keep you there
When the tables turn and it becomes about you instead of
Him.
Pride has been welcomed in
When the invitee comes in you are now on your own,
No Longer protected by
The One who put you on the throne.
You are left alone
To fight with what you see in the mirror.

*Proverbs 30:32-33*

# Follow the Right Leader

It's time to stop playing Follow the leader
Get to know Christ for yourself.
It's time to stop talking about what your pastor said
Know what God said.
If you don't know Christ,
It's time you get a relationship with God for yourself.
When the devil comes with lies
You will know what and whom to believe.
Resist the devil
He will flee.
Always armored,
People will start following
You as you follow Christ.


*2 Timothy 4:3-4*
*1 Corinthians 11:1*

# *I Am Not Ashamed of Jesus Christ*
# *He Leads and I Follow*

I am not ashamed to talk about what I've been through.
Bad decisions I
Helped me become
What God called me to be;
A woman of God,
An ambassador,
A leader to lead others to Christ.
If telling my story
Leads you to Christ
Then my suffering has not been in vain.

*Luke 9:26*
*Revelation 12:11-12*

# Open Your Mouth
## He Deserves the Praise

Open your mouth
Tell somebody what He has done for you
 You don't have to be afraid to tell others
It is your job
Your duty
To give God the praise
The best way to Praise God?
Open your mouth
Tell others what He has done for you.

*Psalm 150:6*
*Revelation 4:11*

# Wisdom-
## God Word is the cure

When you listen with both ears and look with your eyes, you will prevent many negative life lessons. There are some life lessons we are not supposed to learn. The ones that take your eyes and ears away from seeing and hearing God work in your life. When Wisdom speaks, it's time to listen.

God put people in our lives for a reason- to teach us, to help us not repeat mistakes they made. We learn life lessons by watching other people and how they live. The choice is up to you, how you play your part; the world's way of life or God's way of life.

When you don't learn from what you view, you duplicate lessons. Creating a sequel to what you should have learned from the movie you are supposed to be watching.

*Do you want to create a sequel, or do you want to be an original, so people can view your movie?*

**Proverbs 20:12**
**Proverbs 1:20-33**

# Life Is a Teacher

Life is a teacher,
Yes, life is hard.
You make the choices
To make your life better.
The people God placed in your life are placed there for a
reason.
Either you watch the movie
Or let life be your teacher.

*Proverbs 3:13-19*

# You Need to Listen
# If You Are Grown

You don't listen to what just anybody tells you.
What makes you think you're grown?
I've been around long enough to tell you
When wisdom calls you better listen.
Can't you see?
I'm trying to spare you heartache and pain.
If you want to test the water, I won't stop you
Pride comes before Destruction
You have been warned.

*Proverbs 16:18*
*Proverbs 11:2*

# *They Don't Want To Hear What You Say*

They rejected me.
What have I done wrong?
I chose to follow you,
I find your life to be rewarding
Full of Mercy and Grace.
They don't want to hear what I have to say.
They choose to stay away
They still want do things their way.
I'm OK,
I'll keep praying.
One day
They will see things your way.

*1 Thessalonians 4:8*

Carolyn M. Ellison

# *Listen Don't Speak*
## *You Might Miss His Voice*

If God has something to say to you
He will get His point across,
If He has to talk though a donkey.
He speaks to you
You should be quick to listen
slow to speak.
Whatever He has said
You are accountable
For what you heard.

*Numbers 22:28*
*James 1:19*
*Romans 14:12*

## *Cell Phones*

What if there were no cell phones?
OMG what would you do?
Before the cell phone,
Home phones would do.
Never left home until that call you were waiting for came
through.
Now there are cell phones.
You can be reached anywhere.
What if God was like the phone?
Call answered in the order received.
Leave a message please;
Will call you back.
What if there was a black out, and phone calls couldn't go
through?
Thank God, He's not likes the cell phone;
He hears the prayer of the righteous.
All prayers get through.

**Proverbs 15:29**

# God's Wisdom Get Things Done

The fear of the Lord is wisdom.
I fear you Lord,
I fear if I get in your way
The answers I seek will never come.
I fear if I continue
To do things my way
I will continue to get the same result.
I step aside,
 I give it all to you.
I know if I want to see change
I must step aside
Let you do your job.


**Psalm 111:10**

# He Will Test You

I could not wait until I finished school. I never like taking tests. All I wanted to do was have fun. When it was time to take a test, I was not prepared, so I knew the grade I was going to make. I was a good listener, not good enough to retain all that I needed to pass my test.

*Test taking for God requires you to study, and retain all information you learn from each test. Each test you pass allows growth for the next test.*

When we ask God to use our life for His Glory, don't be surprised when the test comes at you. Remember what you asked God to do and use your life. When God's light is shining on you, too much is given, much is required. If you don't retain from each test, you will repeat your test again. If you are a good student, when its promotion time, you will be the star. When we pass test for God, it proves how much you love and trust God.

*Job 23:10*
*Psalm 26:2*
*Genesis 22:1-18*

# *Keep the Answers - They Don't Change*

To teach others
God has to first be your teacher.
Your mind has to be renewed to think like Him,
You must eat the word, and eat what it tells you to do.
Spiritual minded and Carnal minded are not the same.
God creates and man destroys.
When God renews the mind,
Everything about you changes.
With each change comes a test, to see what you learned
from the prior test.
When the enemy attacks the mind
You no longer think in the past
The answers are those which God placed inside you
His words don't change.

*Romans 8:6*
*Luke 6:40*

# Remember What You Asked
# God to Do

Save Me, God
So you can use me for your Glory.
Be careful how you ask God to use you.
To shine in His glory comes with a price.
Expect your life to be turned upside down.
When God showers his glory through you
There will be many tests and trials.
This is not a time to get discouraged or throw in the towel;
You asked God to use you.

*Matthew 16:24*
*Psalm 66:10*
*1 Peter 1:7*

# *What Is Your Motive?*
# *Why Do You Ask?*

You have not because you ask not.
Is it about you?
Or is it about God?
What is in your heart?
Is it for your selfish gain,
Or will God be gloried?
A delay is not a denial
When God is in the center of the reason you are asking.

*James 4:2*

# I Thought I Would Ask

Can I ask you a question?

Well I guess I will ask anyway.

You know what I am about to say.

Can I be selfish today?

Can it be about me for a change?

People know they can depend on me:

I see a need,

I meet the need;

They need to talk,

I am there for them.

What about me?

Can I not be nice today?

Do I have to go church?

Can I stay home?

I know this is a selfish prayer

To think about myself.

I thought I would ask

You already know what's in my heart.

**Psalm 17:3**
**Jeremiah 17:10**

# Do You Know What He Said?

God knows what He said. *He wrote the book.* He wants to see if you know what He said. When you know what He said, you can ask anything in His name. *The only reason you go through changes is because you don't know what His word says to do.*

*Isaiah 55:11*

# *Lord You Said!*

You said!
If I confess
Jesus in my Heart
You will save me from my sins.
You said!
You will give me the desire of my heart
If my desire becomes your desire.
You said!
When I am weak, you are my strength.
You said!
If I wait on you
You will renew my strength.
You said!
You will give me perfect peace if I keep my mind on you.
I have hidden your word in my heart that I may not sin
against you.
You said!
Before your word returns to you void, Heaven and earth will
disappear.

*Romans 10:9*
*Psalm 37:4*
*Psalm 119:11*
*Matthew 24:35*

# Strength-
## People Need to See the God in You

Where are you going to and forth in the land? Have you considered my Servant? Carolyn

God sees what man doesn't see. God knows your beginning and your end. He knows the steps you will take. ***In Your strength you can't do anything. In God's Strength you can do all things.***

God will put your life on display for all to see how you handle your test. If they don't see your story, how would people know what you been through is true? Unless they walked the journey with you to validate what God did in your life.

*Job 1:8*
*Philippians 4:13*
*Ephesians 2:7-10*

# Through Your Eyes, I See Me

Help me to see how you see me.
I feel pain, Lord,
You see me winning the victory.
I see where my life's at,
You see where my life will be.
You see me faithful,
You see me believing,
You see me rejoicing
I have survived all my attacks.
You opened my eyes,
I am healed, I am free.
I am what you see,
Strong and wise.
The storms, the battles
Were not mine to fight.
I couldn't do anything; in my strength.
You give me the capability
To know my story.
You know me,
Validate
The God in me.
All praise, honor and glory
Belong to God.

**Romans 8**

## *Sacrifice-*

Each time we went into the courtroom, I never said a word. He is my lawyer. He will talk for me. This had to be. Yes it hurt, but it hurt God more. I made a small sacrifice for a great reward. To be healed it will take same pain.

*John 18:28-38*
*Genesis 22:2*
*Romans 5:8*

# He Commits the Crime
# I Do the Time

When she strolled into the room, as if she owned it,
no words were spoken.
I'm here for him, not for you.
You sat on the defendant's side
Knife in my heart
Drowning in my own blood.
I eagerly wait your name to be called.
What did I do?
I'm on trial for a crime I didn't commit.
The love of a mother protecting her Daughter.
Instead of you
I get the bullet.

**Psalm 34:17-20**

# *You Don't Know My Pain*

It hurts in many ways
One cannot imagine!
I can't explain the pain.
I know in the end the hurt will be worth it!
I know the cloud that hangs over my head,
Will someday be a ray of sunlight
That sits on a hill and will light up the world.

*1 Peter 4:12-19*
*Revelation 21:4*

# *It Took Pain To Heal Me*

Pain doesn't feel good
By the hands that say
"I love you."
You make me very angry.
Sometimes I wish you hadn't been born.
You cause me nothing but pain.
It took your sting to help me realize
I needed God to heal me.

*Genesis 6:6*
*2 Corinthians 12:9*
*Isaiah 53:5*

# *He Knows What You Can Handle*

He will give you perfect peace
When your mind stays on Him;
When things are out of control
There seems to be no place to go.
His yoke is easy, his burden is light.
Give Him your problems,
Let God fight your fight.

*Isaiah 26:3*
*Matthew 11:30*
*1 Corinthians 10:13*

# *All for My Good*

You see my smile
Not my pain.
I would not change a thing for the wisdom I've gained.
I grew through my pain,
All things work together for the good of those who love the
Lord,
Who have been called by his name.

**Romans 8:28**
**Romans 8:30**

# Stand Still and Watch the Fight

The Lord is my shepherd
He guides me through my fights.
When man tries to destroy me
He will not win the fight,
He will have to go through God
Who's bigger than all.
Because I am His child
I don't have to fear.
He promised to fight my battle
If I stand still.

**Psalms 23:1-6**

# To Be Effective in Helping Others
## One Must Feel Their Pain

I've done things
I am not proud to admit I did.
When you don't want to feel pain, you will do things to
make the pain stop.
I beat myself up by regretting the mistakes.
It took a long time to forgive myself.
I held on to the guilt and the shame
Until you helped me realize it wasn't me who wanted to
hold on to my pain.
It was the devil playing with my mind
He did not want me to forget my pain.
He didn't want me to be healed, to see what you had for me.
That people were to be helped through my trial,
What we go through is not for us.
Tests and trials are to help others
To be affective in helping others…
One must feel the pain.

**Galatians 6:2**
**Luke 10:30-37**

# *Not My Will*
## *But Your Will Be Done*

Lord I am tired,
I cannot take anymore.
You said when I am weak
You will be my strength.
Why do I feel all alone?
When is it going to end?
So many attacks.
My faith is getting weak.
Walking by faith
Seeing what's in my sight,
It's weighs me down.
I know these attacks are from the enemy to get me off track.
Lord I do trust you.
I will continue on my journey
Nevertheless;
Your will be done.

*Mark 14:35-36*
*James 4:10*

# *To Be Healed It Will Hurt*

It was good that I was afflicted.
Pain doesn't feel good during test time;
Through my many tests and trials
I grew to know my strength.
I learned to be content in everything I've been through;
What didn't break me made me strong
The struggle was good for me,
I learned I could survive.

***Psalm 119:71***

# *It Doesn't Hurt Anymore*

I am not tired yet
You will not steal my joy.
I am living to live again.
Do what you may,
I shall not be moved.
I am stronger than that.
You should be tired by now,
All you do is go in circles.
When you know the reason for the attacks
It doesn't hurt anymore.
You can withstand anything the devil throws at you,
His plan won't work.
Greater is He that is in you than anything used against you.


*1 John 4:4*

# *You Keep Me Dry*

Let the rain pour down.
Hurricane
Typhoon,
I won't get wet.
I am covered under your blood.
Pressure of life
Too much for me to contend with,
You made me a promise
I carry it in my heart.
So, let the heavy rain pour down,
I won't get wet.

**Psalm 91:4**

## *Let God Be Your Teacher*

When you are hungry for God; He will feed you. Let Him download His word in you. ***When God gives it nobody can take the word away from you.*** What God has put inside you, people will be amazed of the wisdom you have gained. They will wonder how you got so wise; because they know the old you.

***Don't be surprised if your own people reject you.***

***Luke 2-41:52***
***Matthew 13:54***

# Hidden Treasure

What you learn
No one can take away.
It's kept inside a treasure box
Hidden not far inside.
When the time comes,
The key is given to you,
Only God can unlock the door.
People will be amazed of all the knowledge you gain.
Beware of the doubters, they don't go away
They will remind you of whom you used to be.

*Colossians 2:1-5*
*Isaiah 45:3*

# *The Secret Is for All*

You tell me secrets
Only I can understand.
To these who don't know you,
What I speak is nonsense.
When I say,
"I walk by faith and not by sight,"
That's the secret you told me.
When I say,
"I am more than a conquer
Through Jesus Christ,"
That's the secret you told me.
When I say,
"I walk with the authority, poise and integrity
To be called a child of God,"
That's the secret you told me.
Your secret is available to all who wants to know your
secret.

*1 Corinthians 2:14*
*Jeremiah 29:13*
*Matthew 6:33*

# Envy and Jealousy

What God has for you is for you. What God has for others is for them. *You shouldn't get jealous when you see God blessing people.* People have gone through a lot of tests and trials to get what God has for them. Rejoice for the others. When your time comes, they will rejoice with you. Don't block your blessing by envying other people's blessings.

*James 3:14-16*
*Genesis 37:1-36*
*Romans 12:15*

# *I Did Not Know Why Before Now I Know*

My brothers,
How can you betray me?
You left me to die.
Your jealousy consumed you.
You say I'm Father's favorite,
I was only telling my dream.
Your jealousy caused you to sell me a slave.
I was free.
Through it all, I have found favor in God's sight.
Sent to the palace,
She awaits me.
Lured by her seduction,
I resist.
From the palace to the pit,
Years went by.
Thinking of my father
How to pay you all back.
In the pit I realized this was meant to be.
I was called back to the palace,
I became second in command.
The day I saw you my heart was filled with rage.
The thought of the familiar came running back.
I let Him use me for a moment
To pay you all back.
I am your brother,
Go get Father,

# I Did Not Know Why Before
## Now I Know(Continued)

My home will be your home.
What the devil meant for evil
God meant it for our good.

**Genesis 39-45:19**
**Genesis 50:20**

## *God Has You On A Journey*

While on this journey called life. ***God has called your name.*** He has called you to do some great thing for the kingdom. ***When God calls you, all His plans come with instructions.*** When He called Abram, who name was later change to Abraham God told him to leave his father's house, and home.

***God has a motive and reason for what He has called us to do. We are not to question God.*** He will reveal to you later why He does things His way? Abraham took his nephew Lot with him. It was a distraction. Abraham had to rescue him several times.

When we get out of God's way, **He will do the rescuing.** The more you try to help people who are not ready to change, it brings you down; it's too heavy to carry your weight, and other people's weight.

It takes time away from what God needs to do in your life. God has to do something in you, and get things out of you, so you can go back and help the ones you left behind. ***The blind can't lead the blind.***

***Genesis 12:1;Genesis 14:11-12***

## They Cannot Go With You

When God tells you to leave and don't take anything with
you,
He means just that.
For the journey you're on,
You don't need any distraction.
God has you on a journey all by yourself.
You may not understand why God does and says things
The closer you walk with God –
You will.

*Proverbs 3:5-6*

# *Let Go Of The Baggage*

The baggage has to go!
There are things inside of you that weigh you down.
I cannot use you;
Things of your past.
You don't know how to explain;
I know; I was there.
There's nothing you did that I am not aware of.
I made you.
I knew you would get off the course,
I made another path.
There are many things you must let go of
So I can use you.
People will be watching you.

***Hebrews 12:1***

## *It Will Happen In God time*

There are three hundred sixty-five days in a year; seven days in a week, and twenty-four hours in a day. A second starts time; seconds turn to minutes; minutes turn to hours; hours turn into a day; days turn into weeks; weeks turn into a month; and months turn into years. *We will always wait on time.*

*The hardest thing for us humans to do is to wait.* We are a race of people who has adapted to fast food, the microwave, and the internet. We want everything right now. I don't have time to wait.

When our promises don't come as fast as we think they should, we try help God and the weight gets heavier. *We delay the process* of our waiting on God by adding more weight to what He needs to get out of us to keep the promise. No matter what you do *you cannot rush God.*

If God gives us our promise too soon, would we be able to keep the promise? There are reasons we have to wait on God. So we will learn what it takes to keep the promise and the purpose behind the promise. *There are some things God has to teach us.*

If God makes you a millionaire overnight, how do you

transition out of poverty to riches? *You cannot if you've never been rich.* It will be hard. If all you know how to do is survive; from paycheck to pay check. You will take a poverty mindset, into a millionaire status. You will be broke in no time. Now since you have more, you will spend more. A price tag will have no meaning to your spending.

It is Gods will that we all live in abundances. He wants us to be wise in our spending and giving. A good man leaves an inheritance for his children. To leave an inheritance; a good man knows the importance of wealth; to pass down to his children.

*2 Peter 3:9*
*Proverbs 13:22*

# *God Is Time*

A day is like a thousand years,

A thousand years is like a day to God.

Why do you worry about time?

Abraham was one hundred and Sara was ninety when God

blessed them with their promise.

Time should not matter.

It will come to pass.

You will see your promise.

God is time.


*Psalm 90:4*
*2 Peter 3:8*
*Genesis 17:17*
*Genesis 21:5*

# *Lord The Wait Is Heavy*

Lord you said
Lay aside every weight that holds me down.
It's hard to lay aside the weight when I am waiting on you.
You made me some promises I have been waiting to come
to pass.
It is easy to wait when you know the date.
My date weighs me down
As I wait on my promises.
I know your time is perfect and my date has to wait.
Lord teach me to wait so my strength can be renewed
That I may run and not get weary.
Help me lay aside the weight
As I wait on you.


***Isaiah 40:31***

## Don't Make Promises
## You Cannot Keep

People make promises to the Lord. Once the Lord fulfills the promise, we forget the promise we made to the Lord. You may forget, God doesn't forget. God holds you to your promise.

When we are in distress we will say and do anything, to get what we need from God. Don't think God doesn't already know the motive in your heart. God loves us so much, that He will trust us with His promise.

***When God blesses you with your promise, and you don't make good on your promise, you give God back His promise.***

***Deuteronomy 23:2***

# *Don't Forget Your Promise*
# *You Made to the Lord*

People make promises to the Lord.
When the Lord fulfills the promise;
We get amnesia.
When we are in distress
We will say anything to get God to move.
God knows your heart
If you are telling the truth.
God blesses you
God doesn't
Take His promise back,
You forgot the promise you made.


*Ecclesiastes 5:4*
*Numbers 30:2*

# I Promise to Wait Until I Say "I Do"

Another Friday night.
It's been a long hard week.
What is there to do? Watch TV?
Not enough channels to pass away the time.
It's been five long years,
No human touch.
No artificial touch for me.
I don't need any quick fix.
I choose not to be tempted.
You said you will keep me
If I want to be kept.
Well I do.
You said you will give me the desires of my heart
If I take delight in you.
I made you a promise
To wait until I say "I do."
So I will take a slip, if that's OK with you,
Let the TV watch me fall asleep.

*1 Corinthians 10:13*

# *If He Said It, He Shall Make It Good*

When God makes promises
He doesn't need your help.
He is the creator of the universe,
He owns everything.
He does not need to pull a rabbit out of a hat for you to
believe
He knows what it takes to make your promise come alive.
The promise is not coming fast enough.
You cannot wait on God
You must help fulfill your promise to life.
Now you have created a bigger problem
That takes God to rescue you.
Wait on God.
If He made you a promise,
He will make it good.

*Genesis 17:15-16*
*Genesis 25:12*

# I'm Going To Wait Until My Change Comes

Who can understand my pain?
You, oh Lord!
This deep hollow that hovers over my life.
My soul, drowning in my tears,
No longer reaches the surface.
Where is everyone?
Don't they know
How much my heart bleeds with pain?
All I want to do is love and protect them from the evil one
that waits to enlist their hearts.
Oh Lord, I put my trust in you.
I know you will see me through.
I am going to wait until my change comes.


*Job 14:14*

Carolyn M. Ellison

## *Peace Be Still*

You take my breath away.
It's just you and me
Time and space.
You have a way of getting my attention.
You are my tranquility,
You unwind my soul.
I forget about everything when I am with you.
You make me want to wait in this place.

*Mark 4:39*
*Psalm 107:29*

# Love

No matter what happened to you in your past or who didn't love you, *when you know God's love, you will never settle for another voice other than God's.*

He will teach you how to love and to know when true love comes your way. *When you love yourself, you will know if He loves you.*

For so long I didn't love myself. I did things to get attention and used my body for love. What I thought was love brought painful moments and scars. I never want to feel that kind of painful love again.

When I got my divorce, I made up in my mind that I was going to practice abstinence. By the grace of God it has now been five years. I choose to love me because I don't need anybody else to validate what God has already told me – You are my beautiful daughter. When I look in the mirror, I love me. God has taught me what true love is. It is not what is on the outside; it is what's on the inside that makes you beautiful. *To feel this kind of Love, God has to be your one and only lover.*

*Deuteronomy 6:5*
*1 Corinthians 13:4-7*

# *Teach Me How to Love You*

My past holds me back.
I don't know what true love is.
Mama's rejection,
Daddy's too.
The first man comes along and says, "I love you"
"The love you seek is here."
He's the wrong man if He wasn't sent by God.
Your love is everlasting!
There is no competing for your Love.
Freely you give to those who want to receive.
Teach me how to love you
So I can love myself.

*Psalm 27:10*

# You Don't Have to Wonder

He loves me,
He loves me not.
She loves me,
She loves me not.
When you don't know who you are
You will never know if he or she loves you.
Know God's Love.
When the time comes,
You will know true love.

*John 3:16*
*1 John 4:10*

## *Know Your Self Worth*

Sex should not be a substitution for love.
You are precious in the sight of your Heavenly Father -
A woman of great value
Sweet as an aroma,
With honor and pride.
You're not a bone to toss to dogs.
When you realize your self worth
You will never be tossed again.

*Psalm 139:13-15*

# *You Don't Have to Settle*

Oh taste and see that my lover is good.
I settled before -
Never again.
When you taste true love
You won't ever settle again.
Love comes from within,
Not what you see.
My lover is good to me,
Never abusive.
He never takes from me,
He always gives,
He is not jealous,
He doesn't question me
Where are you going?
Where are you at?

**Psalm 34:8**

# He Is the Lover of My Soul

He is Strong and mighty.

My Man's love is unconditional.

He supplies all my needs,

He never remembers the wrong I did.

He never disrespects me by calling me ugly names.

He cuddles me and tells me all the time how much He loves me.

I don't have to feel guilty being me.

He is available all the time.

He has enough love for all.

Give my Man a try

You won't regret you did.

*John 15:13*

## Heart–to-Heart

Thinking how much I love you,
Your heart and mine
Beating as one.
This feeling
I cannot explain.
One would have to experience
Your love
To know how I feel.
If I should die tonight
I know I will awake in your arms.

**Ezekiel 11:19**

# *Family-*
# *We Have to Love them,*
# *no Matter What*

I love my family. I love when we all get together. When we are all in the same room you can feel the overflow of love as we embrace one another with hugs and kisses.

We as Christians should let the world see the love we have for our family. Our family shouldn't have to reach out to the world for love. Love should start at home first. How can you go out and help save other people, when the ones you left at home are hurting too?

We are to love our family, no matter what condition their lives are in. If we give up on family we might as well give up on God. We cannot give up on helping our family because of their flaws. You cannot change anybody with the mindset of refusing to help them. "They don't want change, and I don't have time help them to change." ***Did God give up on you?*** They may not change as quickly as you would like them to change. When you asked God to change you that's what He did. He changed you.

Your job is to pray and continue loving your family. Love them for who they are. *Your life will be so much lighter if you stop being God to your family.*

When your family can validate who you are in Christ, the world will appreciate the God in you.

*1 Timothy 3:4-5*
*1 Timothy 5:8*
*Gen. 4:8*
*2 Sam. 13*

# *God Chose the Family*

We don't have an option
As to who would be family.
If we did there wouldn't be any excitement.
We would pick family members without any faults - The
perfect family.
We wouldn't care about other people's problems.
If everyone in your family was perfect
How would you know what God can do?
How will you know if God can change their sin?
If everybody was perfect
Why would you need God?

# *Children*

*If we only let them lead the way*. Children are precious gifts from God. Children have a pure heart. God tells us to come to Him as a child. God also tell us how to train up a child. You can teach a child the right way or the wrong way to go. *Children can teach adult so much.* How to *trust*, *love* and to *depend*. They depend on parents for everything, that how God want us to be as a child. When we come to Him.

*Matthew 19:14*

## *Innocence*

Children are a precious gift from God.
To observe a child playing is a beautiful scene.
Their minds are adventurous.
They will create an atmosphere that will illuminate a room.
The warmth of their love; the sweet fragrance they bring
will turn your cloudy day sunny.
If you keep your eyes on these little ones,
The beautiful smiles shine as if the eyes of God are
watching you. Oh!  The example!
If we only let the children lead the way.
If children are our future
It's time we gave them hope
To become the leaders God called them to be.
It's time our children's voices stop crying from the grave.

*Psalm 127:3–5*
*Matthew 19:14*
*Matthew 18:3*
*Philippians 2:15*

# Let Them Go To Grow

**We can train our children in the right way.** To love, trust and fear the consequence; if we don't do what right in the eyes of God. When children get older, they will take on their own identity. They may do things and may disappoint you with things they do... They live a life that you are not pleased with. Their lives are the total opposite of how you raised them. What do you do when you know you raised them up right? And they want to do things their way?

As parents letting our children go is a hard job. If we don't let them go to grow, we will never stop raising children.

If children feel they are grown and ready to leave home, let them go. **You have done your job.** Let them go experience what you are trying to prevent them from going through - life problems.

**There comes a time you need to release them back to God.** No, we don't like to see our love ones suffer; but, they have to go through a process only God can get them through. If we don't stop hindering our loved ones they will never get well. All we can do is pray, pray, and pray and watch the work that God can do in them, so He can get the glory.

*They are not going to stay in the pig pen too long. They will find their way back home.*

*Luke 15:11-32*

# *My Prodigal Child*

There's nothing else I can do for you.
I love you enough to let you go.
The more I help you,
The more I hurt you.
I have had enough,
It's time you were on your own.
You need to find God.
It is He that you need to find.
I trained you up right;
I will sleep at night knowing that he has hedges of
protection over you.
What concerns me, concerns Him.
Let Him teach you.
When You come back
I will see the change; I will see God in you.

# *Runaway Child*

It's a mother's worst nightmare when she doesn't know
where her child is,
The thoughts, the emotions that run through her head.
She may be dying.
She is the most helpless creature on the earth.
Her strength is depleted
Yet, you give her the strength to go on.

# *They Learn From You*

If your child watches your life, and it is not pleasing in the sight of God. You are teaching them it's ok to follow in your footsteps. If you don't know, what you're doing is wrong. How can you teach them? You have allowed your child, to see and hear things, from you, that needs parental guidance.

**Mother-** if your daughters see you pregnant from different men...that is all they know. If they see you cheat on their dad...that is all they know. If your daughters see you dress in ways that reveal your body parts...that is all they know. **Psalm 127:3–5; Titus 2:4**

**Father-**if your sons see you as a deadbeat dad... that is all they know. If they see you beat their mother... that is all they know. If your children see you selling or using drugs, that is all they know. **Ephesians 6:4**

The Bible teaches us how to train up our children. A *godly mother and father* will raise their children up before God, in the instruction given to them by God.

**Godly parents** can rest assured, if you train them up before God, you can go to bed at night knowing God is watching over them.

*Ephesians 5:1–2*
*Deuteronomy 4:9*

# School Starts at Home First

You cannot wait until a child reaches the teen years
To teach them about God.
By this age they have become a student of the street.
That child has developed his or her own identity.
The older that child gets, the harder it is to reach
When they do not hear your voice first.
When children leave home already equipped,
They may encounter many of life's problems.
They may even duplicate what they see.
The word of God said,
"They may stray, but they will be back."
You must instill God at birth.

*Proverbs 22:6*

# *It Doesn't Feel Good Looking at You*

What you plant will grow.
If the seed's not planted on good soil
You will produce a harvest that resembles you.
Monkey see, monkey do.
It doesn't look good when you look at yourself.
When they were looking through your reflection, it was
clear.
My day will come.
Finally, my seeds come alive
That what you plant you don't approve of…
Because it looks so much likes you.

**Galatians 6:7:8**

# Tell Them the Truth

It's time to talk to our children.
It's time keep it real.
Instead of telling them what not to do,
Tell them what happened to you.
Make them understand you are human,
Yes, you made mistakes too.
Because of your mistakes,
Your past led you into places where you did things you are
ashamed of.
It's time for the children to know why you act, and do
The things you do.
If you tell them, it may help them understand you.
Stop making them feel bad. Because no one believed you
It's time to bring to light family secrets,
Stop taking secrets to the grave.
If children know where they come from
It will help them get where they are going.

*Proverbs 12:19*
*John 8:32*
*Zechariah 8:16*

# *Why did my Mama leave me?*

*My Mother could not give me what she did not get.* When you hurt, you cannot see the pain that you cause others. I don't blame my mother for the choices she made. I learned from her mistakes.

*Mark 11:25*
*Ephesians 4:32*
*Isaiah 49:15*

# *Why Did She Leave Me?*

Looked in the cubby
There was nothing to eat.
Where is my mama?
Why did she leave me and my sister all the time?
Street was her home,
No food or light;
Cold winter nights.
Clothes were our heat.
When I looked for mama for a hug,
She was not there.
When I was a child, I acted like a child,
Thought like a child.
Now that I am grown,
I refuse to take my child with me.
I know how it feels to be hungry.
I know how it feels to want a hug,
Mama's not there,
So I cry myself to sleep.
I promise myself if I ever have kids,
They will never live like I did.
They will never go without food or lights.
I will never be the mother
I didn't have.

## *Through Your Eyes I See Your Pain*

I see your pain.
I've been there.
The eyes are a mirror to the soul.
Tears are the cleansing
That helps make us whole.
When I was there,
I wished someone looked into my eyes and saw my cry,
So much pain.
Through it all I was not alone.
You were with me all the time.
I couldn't see you then, because of all my crying.
You dried my tears.
I see clearly now
The pain in your eyes.
Now I am here to help you
Free your soul.

*Hebrews 12:10-11*

# *Death*

There is a season for **birth** and a season for **death**. Life can be painful, so painful, you want to die. I have had much pain in my life; times I just didn't want make it.

I wanted to lie down, go to sleep, and never wake up. I knew God, that didn't make the pain go away. God gave me the strength to press on.

***What you do for Christ will last.*** When earth is no longer your home, when you die, what will people say about you? Did God get the glory from your life?

***When you die, no one should have to preach your eulogy. Your life should tell your story.***

*Ecclesiastes 3:1*
*Psalm 116:8*

# Death Never Came for Me

The last time I was here,
I did not think I was going to make it.
The pain I couldn't bear.
This time the pain is harder,
Harder than before.
I prayed, I cried,
The pain wouldn't go away.
I prayed to die.
For you to take away my pain.
I waited,
I waited,
Death never came.

**Philippians 1:23**

# If You Should Call Me Home

I am surrounded by Death.
Fear has crippled me
Frozen me to the point
I only think of You.
If You should call me home
I know I will awake in your arms,
Surrounded by your host of Angels;
Allured by your beauty,
Never darkness - Only light.
A city that sits on a hill shining bright.
In You I put my trust.
What can man do to me?
He is nothing but a breathe of air.
You give life,
Only you can take it away.

*John 14:1-3*

# *When Death Calls*
# *Will You Be Ready?*

Don't know when.
We all have an appointment.
No rescheduling,
It is a set date.
Only God knows when your time will come.
Will you be ready?
If He calls your name
You decide,
Heaven or Hell.
The choice is yours.
Your possessions,
Glory or fame
Will not be enough to hide you
From where you came
The dust returns to the earth.

*James 4:14*
*Ecclesiastes 3:2*
*Genesis 3:19*

# *I Am Free*

Family, please don't grieve for me.
I am free!
This old earthly body has failed me.
I knocked on Heaven's door,
And God answered
"Come home my child.
Your new Heavenly body will set you free!"
No more suffering,
No more chronic pain,
I am free!
Family when you think of me,
Rejoice; rejoice on the love and happy times we shared.
That may help to ease your pain,
Someday we will meet again.
The only thing I ask
Is that you be ready
If God happens to call your name.
For whatever reason, I had to leave you.
Just know God doesn't make mistakes.
I am free!

# *Now Is the Time to Make Your Reservation Don't Get Left Behind*

While you have time
Make your reservation for heaven
Before it's too late.
Many predictions have been made when the world will
come to end.
Man's predicted dates have come and gone
and earth is still here.
No man knows
When God is coming back
Not even the son or the angel, in heaven.
*Matthew 24:36*

Judgment day will not be a dream.
In a moment, in the twinkling of an eye,
Like a thief in the night
The Lord Himself will descend from Heaven
With a loud trumpet sound.
The dead in Christ will come alive.
*1 Thessalonians 4:16*
*1 Thessalonians 5:1-3*

# Now Is the Time to Make Your Reservation
## Don't Get Left Behind(Continued)

The Bible say to be ready at all times;
Tomorrow not promise to you.
*Matthew 24:44*

You don't have time
To play with your salvation;
Today is the day; to get right with God.
God has given many signs as proof of His sure return.
Judgment day -
Every knee shall bow
Ever tongue will confess
He is  the King of Kings,
Lord of Lords.
*Matthew 12:36*

If you are not ready when God comes back
If your name is not written in the book of life,
You are in trouble.
Heaven won't be your home.
Now is the time to make your reservation.
*Revelation 20:15*

# *Your Final Resting Place*
# *You Choose Your Stay*

When you stand before God
Will you hear Him Say
"Well done?"
Or will you hear,
"Depart from me,
I don't know you."
If you don't repent
And confess the Lord in your heart,
Hell will be your home.

*Matthew 25:41*
*Matthew 25:46*
*Revelation 21:1-27*
*Mark 9:48*
*Revelation 20:10*

## Sow To Reap A Harvest

There was a season in my life when my money was depleted, I didn't have enough to pay my bills. I spent money foolishly. I wasn't mindful that I had a house and a car payment. I was going through a divorce and soon two incomes became one. My mind did not fully transition into the one income and before I knew it, I was getting a foreclosure notice which led to bankruptcy. ***This was an adjustment season for me and I received a serious financial one-on-one class***. Things were really tight for me because I was paying extra bills which I could not afford to pay.

If only I had the mindset back then that I have now! During that season of my life, I became wise with my money. I never stopped paying my tithe. If there was a need in my church or in my family, I would give what I had. I didn't have enough to pay my bills sometimes. So why would I let other people suffer when I could be a help? So why not help lighten other people burdens.

***If you keep a close fist all the time, God cannot put anything in your hand. You have to give to reap...***

*2 Corinthians 9:6-15*
*James 4:17*
*Proverbs 11:24-25*

# *I Sowed My Way Out*

It was a difficult time for me.
I didn't have enough money to pay my bills.
The needs of others were greater than mine.
The money I had, I gave away
To ease the burden of others.
It was a small token to repay
For what He's done for me.
My needs could wait.
He always provides,
Pressed down,
Shaken together,
Running over.
His blessings
Flow in my life.

*Luke 6:38*
*Acts 20:35*
*Hebrews 13:16*

# *Never Be Afraid to Let Go of Something to See What Comes Back*

Never be afraid to let something go to see what you will get back in return.
You'll never know if it was meant for you
If you always keep a tight fist.
If you don't open your hand
Nothing comes in.

***Proverbs 11:24-25***

# No Hard Work Required
# To Make it to the Top

***There are so many get rich pyramid scams.*** The one at the top is the one who gets richer; which is normally the one who starts the pyramid. The ones who are recruited in the pyramid get a piece of the riches, which requires them to work harder than the one at the top. No matter how much you make, the one at the top will always be richer. As you prosper, you make them richer.

***In God, there is no pyramid to climb to get to Him. One step is all it takes. Confess the Lord Jesus as your Savior and that will put you at the top.*** We are all one in God. Salvation is free to all who want to receive. God does not show favoritism. It is His will that everyone make it to the top. However, in order to make it to the top we need each another to survive.

*Romans 10:9*
*Matthew 28:18-20*
*Acts 10:34*
*Romans 12:5*

# *There Is No Ladder to Climb*

God is the head
We are the parts attached to the  head.
There is no ladder to climb.
God does not work on the pyramid system.
We are all promoted equally.
If you get demoted
You are separated from the head.

*1 Corinthians 12*
*Colossians 1:18*

# *All Payment Is Due to God*

People will not let you forget,
What they've done for you.
They hold it over your head,
"You owe me, for what I've done for you."
If you gave from the heart, you already got paid.
If God did not give it to you, you would have it to give.
If we owe anybody
All payment is due to God.

***Romans 13:8***

# He Makes Me Shine

*If God's favor is upon your life, don't let people make you feel guilty for the blessings in your life.* Walk with your head held high. Be a light in the midst of darkness. *They don't know your story* - what it took for you to be in this place with God.

Don't wear hard-times. You don't need to look like what you are going through. People need to see you go through your trial, not wearing your trial. What you go through and how you come out, will determine how many you bring out with you. *Humble yourself under the mighty hand of God. In His time; He will exalt you. God knows who's going to give him the glory.*

*1 Peter 5:6*
*Isaiah 60:1-5*

Carolyn M. Ellison

# *His Light Shines on Me*

The favor of God is upon my life
I will not walk around defeated
I will not wear what I am going through
I will walk with my head held high
Knowing the favor of God shines on my life.


***Psalm 90:17***
***Matthew 5:16***

# He Knows My Name

How wonderful is your name
Ringing throughout the earth.
No one can compare to You.
You created me to be like You.
I am created by a Creator
Who knows my name.

*Isaiah 43:1*
*John 10:14*

# *What Makes Me Independent?*

It's not because I have my own house or my own car.
I am able to pay my bills without help from any man.
Having a mind like Christ gives me the freedom to think for
myself, to be the person He created,
Fearfully and wonderfully made to do all things through
Him who gives me the strength.

***Genesis 2:7***
***Luke 11:28***

# *My Praise Is For Real*

I have so much to be thankful for
When I look back over my life
I should have died many times
The hands of God spared my life
When you see my smile
When you see me worship
When you see me praising Him
It's for real.
I have a lot to thank Him for
He kept me from death
When I didn't have enough sense to let go of my sin.

***Psalm 109:30***
***Psalm 103:1-22***
***Psalm 150:1-6***

# *Number One Fan*

What If you had many fans shouting for You?
The rainbow in the sky would be sweet
Coming together in one harmony.
The world would be a beautiful place to live
If  Your name was advertised, I wouldn't have to ask who
You are
What if this was the day the trumpet sounded?
Who would win the game?
Of course it would be You
It doesn't take a touchdown or a slam Dunk
I will always be your Number One Fan.


**Galatians 2:20**

## *May My Life Speak for Me*

May the work I have done
Speak for me.
May the love that I give
Speak for me.
May the service that I give
Speak for me.
May the life I have lived
Speak for me.
When my work down here is done,
I want to hear You say, "Well done."

*Matthew 25:21*

# *I Am My Father's Child*

Who Am I?
First and foremost
I am my Father's Child.
I am the apple of my Father's eye.
I was created in His image.
Don't I look like my Father?
I walk like *Him*.
I talk like *Him*.
I act like *Him*,
I think like *Him*.
My father and I
Our hearts beat as one
He owns everything;
All the earth and it's fullness belongs to *Him*.
No good thing will *He* withhold from me
If I do what *He* says.
If I profess my big brother Jesus as my Lord and Savior,
If I love and treat people the way I want to be treated.
The life I live is good.
I don't ever want to lose my relationship with my Father.
He makes me love myself;
He makes me smile when I'm feeling blue.
He tells me secrets.
I don't have to wonder what is on *His* mind.
He is my best friend.
In *Him* I can confide.

**1 John 3:10**

# *I Am a Proverbs 31 Woman*

If I brag on Him
Excuse me!
He gives me permission to do and talk about all the things
*He* brought me through.
I am a Proverbs 31 woman!
I survived
rejection, poverty, divorce, bankruptcy,
depression, and a gunshot wound.
Yes, I am blessed!
*He* lives in me.
I can brag on *Him.*
He comes first
My children fall in line.
He changed me, so I can help them.
The beauty in *Him*, illuminates in me.
I use my time wisely to complete *His* missions.
My body is *His* temple -
I am careful what I put in His house.
My home -
His presence is always there.
The resources *He* entrust to me
I use to glorify the kingdom.
When Boaz finds me
He will be the head that follows the one I brag about!

## <u>Invitation to Accept Jesus Christ</u>

The Bible says *"That if thou shalt confess with thy mouth the Lord Jesus, and shalt believe in thine heart that God hath raised him from the dead, thou shalt be saved."* **(Romans 10:9)**

# ABOUT THE AUTHOR

Carolyn. Ellison is a native of Columbia, South Carolina and president and CEO of "Gifts From Above." Her motto is found in **James 1:17**: *"Every good and perfect gift comes from above. "*

Carolyn is the parent of three children and the proud grandmother of nine precious grandchildren.

Carolyn prays *"Words to Live By, Lessons Learned,"* inspires you to examine your life and make much needed life changes.

www.ingramcontent.com/pod-product-compliance
Lightning Source LLC
Chambersburg PA
CBHW030005110426
42736CB00040BA/512